Where We Play Sports

Measuring the Perimeters of Polygons

Greg Roza

PowerMath™

New Hanover County Public Library
201 Chestnut Street
Wilmington, NC 28401

Published in 2004 by The Rosen Publishing Group, Inc.
29 East 21st Street, New York, NY 10010

Book Design: Ron A. Churley

Photo Credits: Cover © Joe McBride/Corbis; p. 5 (left inset) © Reza Estkhrian/Stone; p. 5 (right inset) ©
Yann Arthus-Bertrand/Corbis; pp. 6, 9, 10, 13, 14, 17, 18, 21 by Ron A. Churley; pp. 9 (inset), 14 (inset),
17 (inset) © Mike Powell/Allsport Concepts; p. 10 © Jim Cummings/Taxi; p. 13 (inset) © Robert
Cameron/Stone; p. 18 (inset) © Kindra Clineff/Stone; p. 21 (inset) © Allsport (UK) Limited; p. 22 (left inset)
© Martin Heitner/SuperStock; p. 22 (right inset) by Michael Flynn.

Library of Congress Cataloging-in-Publication Data

Roza, Greg.
    Where we play sports : measuring the perimeters of polygons /
Greg Roza.
        p. cm. — (PowerMath)
    Includes index.
    Summary: Discusses how to measure the perimeters of vari-
ous types of playing fields, such as football and soccer, by using
addition and multiplication.
    ISBN 0-8239-8972-0 (lib. bdg.) — ISBN 0-8239-8895-3 (pbk.)
    6-pack ISBN: 0-8239-7423-5
    1. Mensuration—Juvenile literature. 2. Perimeters (Geometry)
—Juvenile literature. 3. Polygons—Juvenile literature. 4.
Science
—Experiments—Juvenile literature.   [1. Measurement. 2. Perimeters (Geometry) 3. Polygons.]   I. Title. II. Series.
QA465.R699 2004
516—dc21

2002153792

Manufactured in the United States of America

Contents

What Is a Polygon?

A **polygon** is a closed shape with three or more straight sides and three or more **angles**. A triangle is a polygon. Squares and rectangles are polygons, too. A circle is not a polygon because it does not have angles or straight sides.

The sides and angles of a polygon do not need to be equal. A shape is a polygon as long as each of its sides meets up with exactly two other sides.

Our world is filled with many kinds of polygons. For example, a pool table is a rectangle, which is one kind of a polygon. Many swimming pools are rectangles, too.

swimming pool

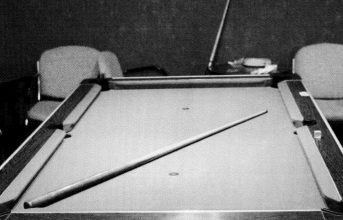

pool table

The word "polygon" comes from the Greek language. It means "many knees" or "many angles."

2 inches

2 inches

4 inches

2 inches

Do the Math

Perimeter of a square		or:
	2 inches	
	2 inches	2 inches
	2 inches	x 4 sides
	+ 2 inches	**8 inches**
a perimeter of **8 inches**		

Perimeter of a rectangle	
	4 inches
	4 inches
	2 inches
	+ 2 inches
a perimeter of **12 inches**	

What Is Perimeter?

Perimeter is the measure of the **distance** around a closed shape. A square has four equal sides. If one side of a square is 2 inches long, each of the other sides is also 2 inches long. To find the perimeter, just add 2 + 2 + 2 + 2. You could also multiply 2 by 4 to find the answer.

A rectangle has two opposite sides that are long and two opposite sides that are short. If one short side of a rectangle is 2 inches, and one long side is 4 inches, what is the perimeter of the rectangle?

Since we know this shape is a rectangle, we also know that both long sides are 4 inches long and both short sides are 2 inches long. So the perimeter is 4 + 4 + 2 + 2, or 12 inches.

A Basketball Court

We can use what we know about polygons and perimeters to talk about the places where we play sports. Basketball is a sport played on a **rectangular** court that is usually made of wood or **asphalt**. Two teams of 5 players each must try to throw the basketball through a basket. While each team tries to throw the ball, the other team tries to stop them.

Most high school basketball courts are 84 feet long and 50 feet wide. What is the perimeter of a high school basketball court? To find out, add 84 + 84 + 50 + 50. Look at the math box on page 9 to find the answer.

50 feet

84 feet

Do the Math

Perimeter of a basketball court	84 feet
	84 feet
	50 feet
	+ 50 feet
a perimeter of 268 feet	

9

53 yards

120 yards

END ZONE

Goal Line

G 10 20 30 40 50 40 30 20 10 G

Goal Line

END ZONE

Do the Math

Perimeter of a
football field

1
120 yards
120 yards
53 yards
+ 53 yards

a perimeter of **346 yards**

A Football Field

Football is played on a football field by two teams of 11 players each. To score points, a team must get the football past the other team's goal line. The team can do this by throwing the ball to a person in the **end zone** or running with the ball into the end zone. A team can also score by kicking the ball between two posts in the end zone. The team without the ball must try to stop the team with the ball.

A football field is usually a rectangle that is 120 yards long and 53 yards wide. What is the perimeter of a football field? You can figure it out by adding 120 + 120 + 53 + 53. Look at the math box on page 10 to find the answer.

A Baseball Diamond

Baseball is played by two teams of 9 players each. Each team has a pitcher who throws the ball. One at a time, the players on the other team try to hit the ball with a bat. After a batter hits the ball, they try to score a point, or **run**, for their team by running around the baseball diamond.

The field is called a diamond because of its shape: it is a square standing on one corner. The corner where the batter stands to hit the ball is called home plate. The other three corners are called bases. The distance between bases on a baseball diamond is 90 feet. To find the perimeter of the diamond, add 90 + 90 + 90 + 90. You could also multiply 90 by 4. Look at the math box on page 13 to find the answer.

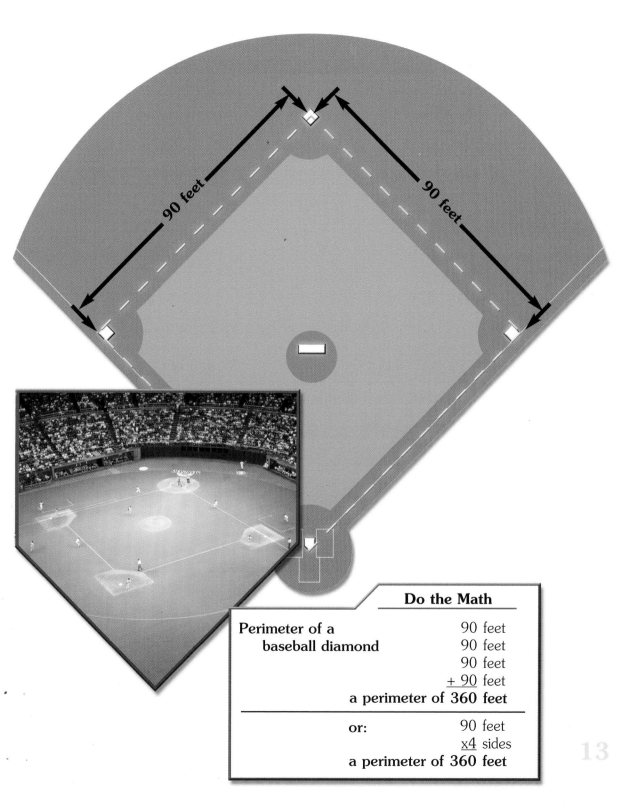

90 feet

90 feet

Do the Math

Perimeter of a baseball diamond	90 feet
	90 feet
	90 feet
	+ 90 feet
a perimeter of **360 feet**	

or:	90 feet
	x4 sides
a perimeter of **360 feet**	

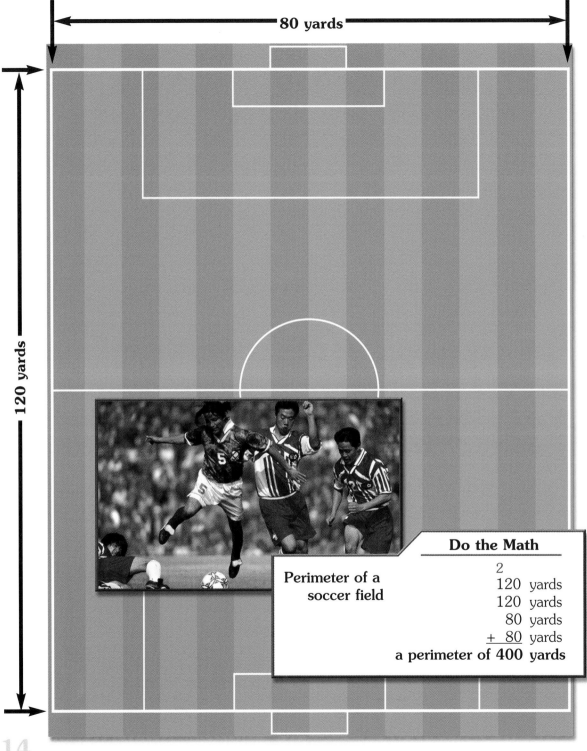

80 yards

120 yards

Perimeter of a
soccer field

Do the Math

$$\begin{array}{r} 2 \\ 120 \text{ yards} \\ 120 \text{ yards} \\ 80 \text{ yards} \\ \underline{+\ \ 80} \text{ yards} \end{array}$$

a perimeter of 400 yards

14

A Soccer Field

Soccer is a sport played on a soccer field by two teams of 11 players each. Each team must try to kick the soccer ball past the other team and into a large net called a goal. Players cannot touch the ball with their hands. They must kick the ball or bounce it off their heads. Each team has a **goalie**, who protects the goal. Goalies are the only players allowed to touch the ball with their hands.

The soccer field used by major teams is a rectangle that is 120 yards long and 80 yards wide. To find the perimeter, add 120 + 120 + 80 + 80. Look at the math box on page 14 to find the answer.

A Tennis Court

Tennis is a sport played by 2 or 4 people on a rectangular court. Tennis players use **rackets** to hit a tennis ball back and forth over a net. A player scores points if their **opponent** cannot hit the ball back over the net or if their opponent hits the ball outside of the court.

In singles tennis, there is 1 person on each side of the net. In doubles tennis, there are 2 people on each side of the net. A singles tennis court is 78 feet long and 27 feet wide. To find the perimeter, add 78 + 78 + 27 + 27. A doubles tennis court is also 78 feet long, but it is 36 feet wide. To find the perimeter of both courts, look at the math box on page 17.

36 feet

78 feet

Doubles Court

Do the Math

Perimeter of a singles tennis court	
	3
	78 feet
	78 feet
	27 feet
	+ 27 feet
a perimeter of **210 feet**	

Perimeter of a doubles tennis court	
	2
	78 feet
	78 feet
	36 feet
	+ 36 feet
a perimeter of **228 feet**	

60 yards

110 yards

Goal

Do the Math

Perimeter of a lacrosse field	
	1
	110 yards
	110 yards
	60 yards
	+ 60 yards
a perimeter of	**340 yards**

Perimeter of a lacrosse goal	
	6 feet
	x 4 sides
a perimeter of	**24 feet**

A Lacrosse Field

Lacrosse is played on a rectangular field by two teams of either 10 or 12 players each. Players use a long stick with a net on the end of it to carry and throw a small, hard ball. Each team tries to score points by throwing the ball into a goal. At the same time, they try to stop the other team from scoring.

A lacrosse field is 110 yards long and 60 yards wide. To find the perimeter, you can add 110 + 110 + 60 + 60.

A lacrosse goal is a net attached to a square frame that is 6 feet high and 6 feet wide. To find the perimeter, you can multiply 6 feet by 4. Look at the math box on page 18 for the answer.

Playing Field Hockey

Field hockey is played on a rectangular field by two teams of 11 people each. Each team must try to score by hitting a small, hard ball into a goal with their curved sticks. They must also try to stop the other team from scoring.

A field hockey field is 100 yards long and 60 yards wide. To find the perimeter, add 100 + 100 + 60 + 60.

What is the perimeter of a field hockey field in feet? There are 3 feet in a yard. Multiply 320 yards by 3 feet. Check the math box on page 21 for the answer.

Do the Math

Perimeter of a
field hockey field

$$
\begin{array}{r}
1 \\
100 \text{ yards} \\
100 \text{ yards} \\
60 \text{ yards} \\
+\ 60 \text{ yards} \\
\hline
\end{array}
$$

a perimeter of **320 yards**

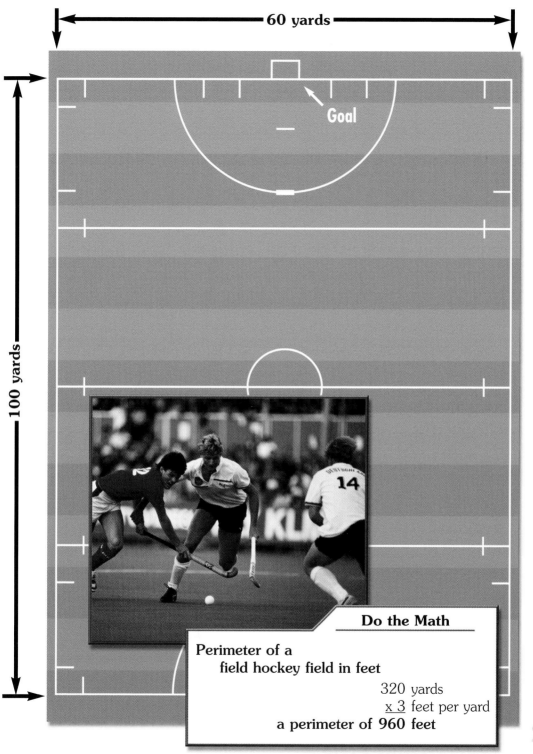

60 yards

100 yards

Goal

Do the Math

Perimeter of a
   field hockey field in feet

       320 yards
    <u>x 3</u> feet per yard
a perimeter of 960 feet

Perimeters off the Field

Sports fields aren't the only polygons with perimeters we can measure. If you were building a swimming pool in your backyard, you would first need to figure out the perimeter of the pool to see if you had enough room. If you were shopping for a new rug, you would need to know the perimeter of the room to know what size rug to get. Whether you're on the field or off, it helps to know how to measure perimeters.

Glossary

angle (AIN-guhl) A corner formed where two straight lines meet.

asphalt (AS-fahlt) A mixture of tar, crushed rock, and sand that can be used to make roads and sports surfaces.

distance (DISS-tuhns) A measure of length.

end zone (END ZOHN) The area beyond the goal line on a football field.

goalie (GOH-lee) The player on a team who guards the goal.

opponent (uh-POH-nuhnt) The player or team against whom you or your team is playing.

perimeter (puh-RIH-muh-tuhr) The measure of the distance around a closed shape.

polygon (PAH-lee-gahn) A closed shape with three or more angles and three or more straight sides.

racket (RA-kuht) An oval frame with strings tied tightly across it, used to play sports like tennis.

rectangular (rek-TANG-gyuh-luhr) A word describing something that is shaped like a rectangle.

run (RUHN) A point scored in baseball by running all the way around the bases.

Index